THE SUN
and Its Patterns

by Thomas K. Adamson

PEBBLE
a capstone imprint

Published by Pebble, an imprint of Capstone.
1710 Roe Crest Drive, North Mankato, Minnesota 56003
capstonepub.com

Library of Congress Cataloging-in-Publication Data is available on the Library of Congress website.

ISBN: 9781666355024 (hardcover)
ISBN: 9781666355062 (paperback)
ISBN: 9781666355109 (ebook PDF)

Summary: What is the sun? Why do we have seasons? What are eclipses? Discover the science behind the sun and its patterns as you answer these questions and more.

Editorial Credits
Editor: Alison Deering; Designer: Sarah Bennett; Media Researcher: Svetlana Zhurkin; Production Specialist: Katy LaVigne

Image Credits
Capstone Studio: Karon Dubke, 21; Shutterstock: Alexandros Michailidis, 15 (right), BlueRingMedia, 18, D1min, 4–5, Designua, 13, Jag_cz, 6, kesipun, 11, Mrs. Nuch Sribuanoy, 1, Nasky, 14, Nuttapong Takote, 20, Patrick Foto, 10, Rushvol, 8–9, S.Borisov, 12, SAPhotog, 15 (left), ScottyJ3785, 19, TommyBrison, 16–17, TTstudio, cover, Vibrant Image Studio, 4 (top left) and throughout, Vladimir Arndt, 7

All internet sites appearing in back matter were available and accurate when this book was sent to press.

Table of Contents

Words in **bold** are in the glossary.

What Is the Sun?

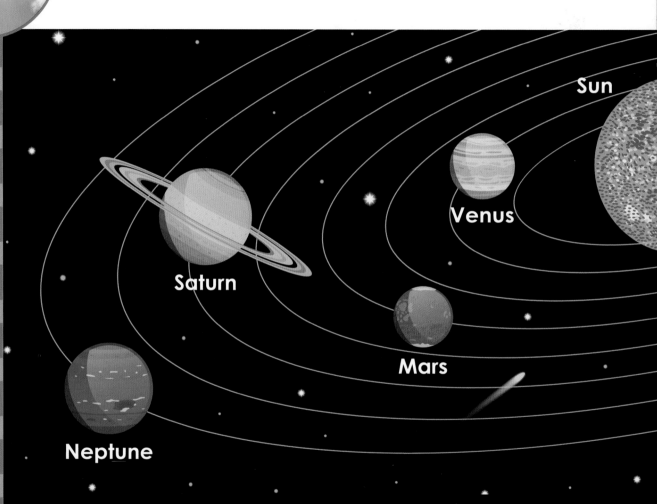

Sun

Venus

Saturn

Mars

Neptune

solar system

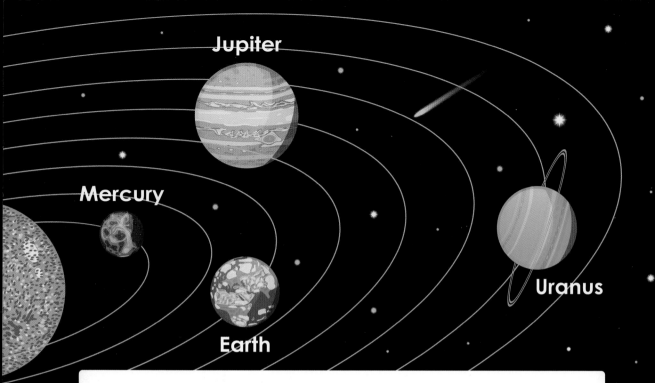

The sun is a **star**. Stars are huge balls of bright, hot gases. They make their own heat and light.

The sun is the closest star to Earth. It is at the center of the **solar system**. Our solar system is made up of the sun, planets, and everything that moves around it.

How Far Away Is the Sun?

The sun is about 93 million miles (150 million kilometers) away from Earth. If you could fly there in an airplane, it would take more than 19 years!

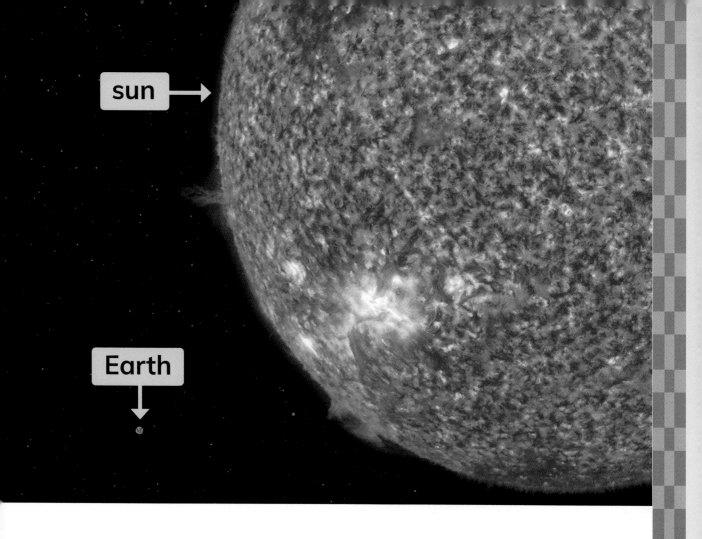

sun →

Earth

The sun is by far the largest thing in our solar system. Imagine the sun is the size of a basketball. In comparison, Earth is no larger than the head of a pin.

Why Does the Sun Rise in One Place and Set in Another?

The sun seems to move across the sky. It rises in the east. At night, it sets in the west. The sun isn't moving. We are!

Earth spins on its **axis**. It **rotates** to the east. That's what makes the sun rise and set.

Why Are Mornings Usually Colder than Afternoons?

The sun warms Earth's surface as it rises. But it doesn't happen all at once. As the hours pass, **temperatures** rise. That's why afternoons are usually the warmest part of the day.

Once the sun sets, heat leaves the surface. The temperature drops through the night.

Why Do We Have Seasons?

Earth's axis is tilted. But it always points in the same direction. Because Earth moves around the sun, different places get more direct sunlight at different times of the year. If Earth's axis was not tilted, the seasons would never change.

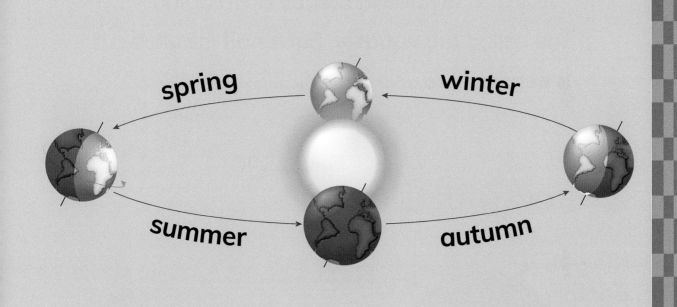

spring

winter

summer

autumn

Earth rotating around the sun

Why Is Summer Warmer than Winter?

Earth is divided in half by an imaginary line called the **equator**. Each half is called a **hemisphere**.

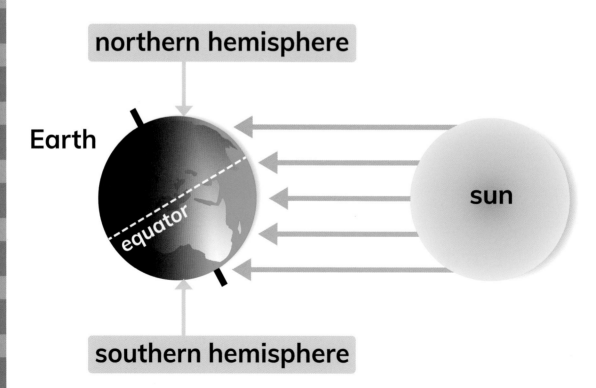

northern hemisphere

Earth

equator

sun

southern hemisphere

July in South Africa   **July in Europe**

When the northern hemisphere leans away from the sun, it's colder. That's winter. During summer, it leans toward the sun. The opposite happens in the southern hemisphere.

Why Are Days Longer in Summer?

The hemisphere tilted toward the sun gets more direct sunlight. That means longer, brighter days. In summer, the sun rises earlier and sets later in the northern hemisphere.

Day and night are always 12 hours long at the equator. Without Earth's tilted axis, everywhere would have equal day and night.

What Are Eclipses?

Sometimes, the moon moves between the sun and Earth. The moon casts its shadow on Earth. That causes a **solar eclipse**.

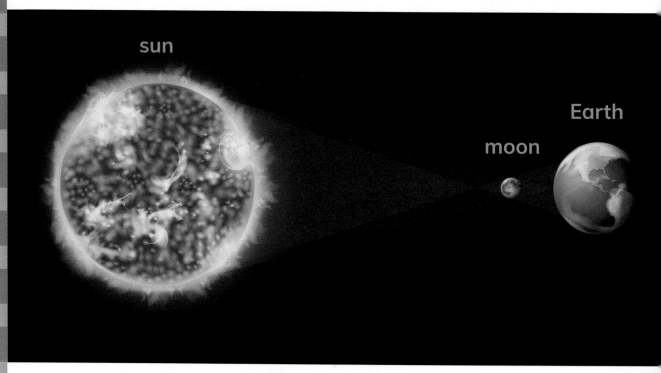

sun

moon

Earth

solar eclipse

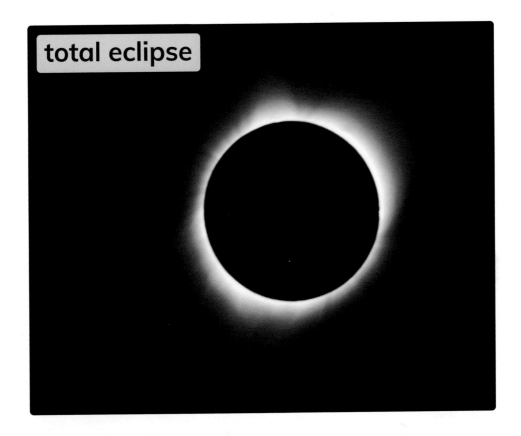

total eclipse

In a total eclipse, the moon blocks the sun completely. The sky becomes dark as night for a few minutes. In a partial eclipse, the moon doesn't completely cover the sun.

Sun Shadows

Measure a shadow at different times of the day to see the sun's pattern of movement across the sky.

What You Need

- a paved area
- 1 other person
- sidewalk chalk
- tape measure
- notebook and pencil
- clock or watch

What You Do

1. Go to a driveway or another paved area on a sunny day.

2. Have the other person stand very still.

3. Using sidewalk chalk, draw the outline of the other person's shadow on the pavement.

4. Measure how long the shadow is from top to bottom.

5. Write down what time it is and the length of the shadow.

6. Two hours later, repeat steps 2-5. Do this again at least two more times throughout the day.

How does the shadow change throughout the day? Does it get longer or shorter as the day goes on? Remember that the sun is low in the sky in the morning and at the end of the day. The sun is high in the sky at noon. How does that affect the shadow?

Glossary

axis (AK-siss)—a real or imaginary line through the center of an object, around which the object turns

equator (ih-KWAY-tuhr)—an imaginary line around the middle of Earth; it divides the northern and southern hemispheres

hemisphere (HEM-uhss-fihr)—one half of Earth; the equator divides Earth into northern and southern hemispheres

rotate (ROH-tate)—to spin around; Earth rotates once every 24 hours

solar eclipse (SOH-lur ih-KLIPSS)—a period of daytime darkness when the moon passes between the sun and Earth

solar system (SOH-lur SISS-tuhm)—the sun and the objects that move around it; our solar system has eight planets, dwarf planets including Pluto, and many moons, asteroids, and comets

star (STAR)—a large ball of burning gases in space

temperature (TEM-pur-uh-chur)—the measure of how hot or cold something is

Read More

Kingston, Seth. *Eclipses*. New York: PowerKids Press, 2021.

Leed, Percy. *Sun: A First Look*. Minneapolis, MN: Lerner Publications, 2023.

Maurer, Tracy Nelson. *Seasons*. New York: Crabtree Publishing, 2022.

Internet Sites

NASA Science Solar System Exploration: Sun
solarsystem.nasa.gov/solar-system/sun/overview

NASA Space Place: What Is a Solar Eclipse?
spaceplace.nasa.gov/eclipse-snap/en

SciJinks: Why Does Earth Have Seasons?
scijinks.gov/earths-seasons

Index

About the Author

Thomas K. Adamson has written lots of nonfiction books for kids. Sports, math, science, cool vehicles—a little of everything! When not writing, he likes to hike, watch movies, eat pizza, and of course, read. Tom lives in South Dakota with his wife, two sons, and a Morkie named Moe.